TARTS

MARKS &
SPENCER

TARTS

SARAH BANBERY

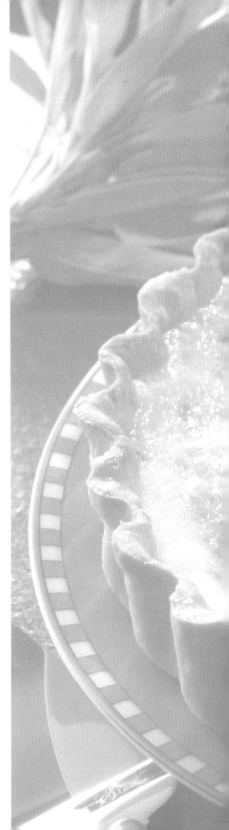

Marks and Spencer p.l.c.
PO Box 3339, Chester CH99 9QS

T21/7688/5306D

www.marksandspencer.com

ISBN: 1-84461-027-6

Printed in China

Produced by the Bridgewater Book Company Ltd

Photographer: David Jordan

Home Economist: Jacqueline Bellefontaine

Notes for the Reader

This book uses both metric and imperial measurements. Follow the same units of measurement throughout; do not mix metric and imperial. All spoon measurements are level: teaspoons are assumed to be 5 ml, and tablespoons are assumed to be 15 ml. Unless otherwise stated, milk is assumed to be full fat, individual vegetables such as potatoes are medium, and pepper is freshly ground black pepper. Recipes using raw or very lightly cooked eggs should be avoided by infants, the elderly, pregnant women, convalescents and anyone suffering from an illness. The times given are an approximate guide only. Preparation times differ according to the techniques used by different people and the cooking times may also vary from those given. Optional ingredients, variations or serving suggestions have not been included in the calculations.

Picture acknowledgments
The Bridgewater Book Company would like to thank Corbis Images for permission to reproduce copyright material on pages 6, 8, 30, 52, 74.

CONTENTS

Tarts are a food of infinite variety and possibility, which can be simple and satisfying or elegant and refined – either way they are always a pleasure to make and eat.

This book contains a collection of tarts for every occasion, whether an intensely flavoured two-bite morsel with a cocktail or a deeply impressive tart of fine sophistication. The tart is the simplest and most self-contained form of food and can be dressed up or down. Being eminently portable, it makes a perfect choice for a picnic and is never out of place, even at a celebration dinner party. A tart is always appropriate, whatever the occasion.

The possibilities are endless, not only for the filling but also for the pastry: you can add a whole variety of ingredients to a basic pastry to enhance and complement the filling – herbs, spices and cheese are great additions to savoury tarts and make the pastry every bit as important

INTRODUCTION

as what it holds. Tarts are also superb if you are planning ahead, as a pastry case can be made well in advance and frozen until needed.

You will find a wide variety of tarts here, sweet and savoury, large and small but above all, smart, sophisticated and modern.

A NOTE ON PASTRY

The following tips, which apply to all the recipes, will help make your pastry a success every time:

• Allow a little more butter and flour than the amount stated in the recipe, extra flour for rolling out the pastry and a little additional butter to grease the tart tin.

• Always roll out the pastry and line the tin before chilling, as this will stop the pastry from shrinking. In this way you can trim the pastry edges before baking to give a neat finishing edge. Always chill pastry before cooking.

• Keep the raw pastry trimmings to plug any cracks or small holes which may appear after baking the tart blind. Simply press a little of the raw pastry into the crack and the heat of the cooked pastry will fix it in place.

• Preheat the oven with a heavy baking tray in it on which the tart case can be placed. This will cook the pastry better and makes it easier to get the tart in and out of the oven.

• To bake blind, use baking paper, which you can scrunch up and then smooth out to fit into the tart snugly.

• All the recipes use large eggs.

• The butter and water for the pastry should always be as cold as possible and the flour should always be sifted.

• If not using a food processor simply sift the flour and salt into a large bowl and rub in the butter by hand.

• Almost all the large tarts in this book could be adapted to make six or eight individual tarts.

• Pastry can be made in advance, frozen, then defrosted before use.

Individual tartlets served as a first course or light lunch are something rather special. A little more labour-intensive than a single large tart, they are more than worth the trouble as they look fabulous and always impress. One of the advantages of tart-making is that the pastry can be made then either chilled, frozen or cooked ahead of time, which gives great flexibility. Small tartlets can be thawed, filled and cooked in minutes.

Canapé or hors d'oeuvre-type tartlets can be made ahead of time and look pretty presented

PART ONE
AN INDIVIDUAL APPROACH

A MIXTURE OF FIRST-COURSE INDIVIDUAL AND COCKTAIL-SIZE TARTLETS

on a large tray. Once you have made your pastry shells you can let your imagination run wild and fill them with a wonderful mixture of fillings – a great opportunity to create new, unexpected and imaginative flavour combinations.

With smaller tarts the pastry works as a background to the fillings so it needs to be crisp but also substantial enough to be held in the hand without crumbling. This is most important when making tartlets for parties. The fillings for the tartlets must not make the pastry soggy so the tartlets must either be baked with their filling and left to go cold or the cases baked ahead, with their filling added just before serving.

CATALAN PIMENTO TARTLETS

MAKES 12 TARTLETS

Pastry

225 g/8 oz plain flour

pinch of salt

100 g/3¹/2 oz cold butter, cut into pieces

cold water

Filling

1 large red pepper or bottled pimento

100 g/3¹/2 oz chorizo dulce sausage, chopped into small pieces

pinch of sweet smoked paprika

salt and pepper

2–3 tbsp tomato purée

240 ml/9 fl oz double cream

¹/2 tsp saffron

2 egg yolks

Lightly butter a 7.5-cm/3-inch, 12-hole muffin tray. Sift the flour and salt into a food processor, add the butter and process until the mixture resembles fine breadcrumbs. Tip the mixture into a large bowl and add a little cold water, just enough to bring the dough together. Turn out on to a floured surface and cut the dough in half. Roll out the first piece and cut out 6 x 9-cm/ 3¹/2-inch circles. Take each circle and roll out to 12 cm/4³/4 inches diameter and line the muffin holes, pressing to fit. Repeat with the remaining dough. Line the pastry with baking paper and baking beans and then put into the refrigerator to chill for 30 minutes. Meanwhile, preheat the oven to 200°C/400°F/Gas Mark 6.

While the pastry is chilling, either grill or roast the red pepper whole until the skin has blackened and the flesh is soft. Cool slightly and peel, discarding the seeds and stalk, then slice the pepper into thinnish strands (if using bottled pimento simply drain and slice). Heat a non-stick

USING A MUFFIN TIN RATHER THAN AN ORDINARY TARTLET TIN MAKES FOR DECENT-SIZED TARTLETS. THE PASTRY TENDS TO SHRINK LESS AS YOU CAN BAKE THE TARTLET SHELLS BLIND BEFORE ADDING THE FILLING. IF YOU DON'T WANT TO BAKE THE TARTLETS BLIND PUT THE LINED TIN IN THE FREEZER FOR 30 MINUTES BEFORE COOKING.

frying pan and fry the chorizo sausage until just browning, add the paprika and season with salt and pepper. Stir for about 1 minute then remove from the heat.

Remove the muffin tray from the refrigerator and bake the tartlets blind for 10 minutes in the preheated oven, then carefully remove the paper and beans.

Spoon a little tomato purée into each tartlet and divide the red pepper and chorizo among them. Put the cream and saffron into a small saucepan and heat to just below simmering point. Beat the egg yolks in a bowl and pour the hot cream over them, whisking to combine. Divide the custard among the tartlets and bake for 10–15 minutes, until just set.

SMOKED SALMON, DILL & HORSERADISH TARTLETS

MAKES 6 TARTLETS

Pastry

125 g/4^1/2 oz plain flour

pinch of salt

75 g/2^1/2 oz cold butter, cut into pieces

cold water

Filling

120 ml/4 fl oz crème fraîche

1 tsp creamed horseradish

^{1}/2 tsp lemon juice

1 tsp Spanish capers, chopped

salt and pepper

3 egg yolks

200 g/7 oz smoked salmon trimmings

bunch fresh dill, chopped

Butter 6 x 9-cm/3^1/2-inch loose-bottomed fluted tart tins. Sift the flour and salt into a food processor, add the butter and process until the mixture resembles fine breadcrumbs. Tip the mixture into a large bowl and add a little cold water, just enough to bring the dough together. Turn out on to a floured surface and divide into 6 equal-sized pieces. Roll each piece to fit the tart tins. Carefully fit each piece of pastry in its case and press well to fit the tin. Roll the rolling pin over the tin to neaten the edges and trim the excess pastry. Cut 6 pieces of baking paper and fit a piece into each tart, fill with baking beans and chill in the refrigerator for 30 minutes. Meanwhile, preheat the oven to 200°C/400°F/Gas Mark 6.

Bake the tart cases blind for 10 minutes in the preheated oven then remove the beans and baking paper.

Meanwhile, put the crème fraîche, horseradish, lemon juice, capers and salt and pepper into a bowl and mix well. Add the egg yolks, the smoked salmon and the dill and carefully mix again. Divide this mixture among the tart cases and return to the oven for 10 minutes. Cool in the tins for 5 minutes before serving.

OTHER HERBS CAN BE SUBSTITUTED FOR DILL. TARRAGON, LEMON BALM OR CORIANDER WOULD ALSO WORK WELL. FOR A SPECIAL OCCASION YOU COULD ADD ^{1}/2 TSP CRÈME FRAÎCHE, 1 TSP BLACK LUMPFISH ROE AND A LITTLE SPRIG OF DILL TO EACH TART JUST BEFORE SERVING.

BALSAMIC DUCK & RADICCHIO TARTLETS

MAKES 12 TARTLETS

Pastry

225 g/8 oz plain flour

pinch of salt

100 g/3½ oz cold butter, cut into pieces

½ tsp icing sugar

cold water

Filling

2 Gressingham duck breasts

pinch of salt

25g/1 oz butter

1 tbsp olive oil

2 onions, thinly sliced

2 tsp soft brown sugar

1 tbsp aged balsamic vinegar of Modena, plus extra for drizzling

salt and pepper

½ large or 1 small radicchio, trimmed and thinly shredded

flat-leaved parsley, chopped

Butter a 7.5-cm/3-inch, 12-hole muffin tray. Sift the flour and salt into a food processor, add the butter and process until the mixture resembles fine breadcrumbs. Tip the mixture into a large bowl, stir in the sugar and add a little cold water, just enough to bring the dough together. Turn out on to a floured surface and cut the dough in half. Roll out the first piece and cut out 6 x 9-cm/3½-inch circles. Next take each circle and roll out to 12 cm/4½ inches diameter and fit into the muffin holes, pressing to fit. Do the same with the remaining dough. Put a piece of baking paper in each hole and then fill with baking beans. Put the tray in the refrigerator to chill for 30 minutes. Meanwhile, preheat the oven to 200°C/400°F/Gas Mark 6.

Remove the muffin tray from the refrigerator and bake the tartlets blind for 10 minutes in the preheated oven, then carefully remove the paper

READY-COOKED CHINESE DUCK WOULD ALSO WORK WELL IF RE-HEATED AND SHREDDED. THERE ARE MANY OPTIONAL GARNISHES FOR THESE TARTLETS, SUCH AS A FEW THIN STRIPS OF ORANGE ZEST, OR SUBSTITUTE SOY SAUCE FOR THE BALSAMIC VINEGAR: SIMMER UNTIL THICK, DRIZZLE OVER THE DUCK AND TOP WITH SHREDDED SPRING ONION.

and beans and return to the oven for a further 5 minutes. Cool in the tin until cold, and leave the oven on.

Wipe the duck breasts, make a series of thin, diagonal cuts in the skin and rub in a little salt. Place the duck on a rack set over a roasting tin and roast for 25–30 minutes, until crisp. Meanwhile, heat the butter and olive oil in a frying pan and add the onions and sugar and cook gently for 20–25 minutes, until soft and slightly caramelized. Add the balsamic vinegar, salt and pepper and the radicchio and cook for a further 5 minutes. Remove the duck from the oven and rest for 5 minutes.

Place the tartlet cases on a serving dish and spoon in the onion and radicchio. Slice the duck very thinly and divide among the tarts. Sprinkle with the parsley and drizzle with a little more balsamic vinegar. Serve warm.

CHERRY TOMATO
& POPPY SEED TARTLETS

MAKES 12 TARTLETS

Pastry

225 g/8 oz plain flour

pinch of salt

100 g/3½ oz cold butter, cut into pieces

2 tsp poppy seeds

cold water

Filling

24 cherry tomatoes

1 tbsp olive oil

25 g/1 oz unsalted butter

25 g/1 oz plain flour

270 ml/9 fl oz milk

salt and pepper

50 g/1¾ oz mature Cheddar cheese

100 g/3½ oz cream cheese

12 fresh basil leaves

Lightly butter a 7.5-cm/3-inch, 12-hole muffin tray. Sift the flour and salt into a food processor, add the butter and process until the mixture resembles fine breadcrumbs. Tip the mixture into a large bowl and add the poppy seeds and a little cold water, just enough to bring the dough together. Turn out on to a floured surface and cut the dough in half. Roll out the first piece and cut out 6 x 9-cm/3½-inch circles. Take each circle and roll out to 12 cm/4½ inches diameter and fit into the muffin holes, pressing to fill the holes. Do the same with the remaining dough. Put a piece of baking paper in each hole and fill with baking beans then put the tray in the refrigerator to chill for 30 minutes. Meanwhile, preheat the oven to 200°C/400°F/Gas Mark 6.

Remove the muffin tray from the refrigerator and bake the tartlets blind for 10 minutes in the preheated oven, then carefully remove the paper and beans. Put the tomatoes in an oven tray, drizzle with the olive oil, and roast for 5 minutes.

Melt the butter in a saucepan, stir in the flour and cook for 5–8 minutes. Gradually add the

milk, stirring to combine into a white sauce. Cook for a further 5 minutes. Season well with salt and pepper and stir in the cheeses until well combined. Put 2 tomatoes in each tart case and spoon in the cheese sauce, then put back into the oven for 15 minutes. Remove from the oven and top each tartlet with a basil leaf.

OTHER INGREDIENTS COULD BE ADDED TO THESE TARTS, SUCH AS ½ AN ANCHOVY IN EACH ONE BEFORE ADDING THE CHEESE SAUCE, OR A FEW CHOPPED HERBS. CHEESE PASTRY WOULD ALSO WORK WELL: SIMPLY ADD 50 G/2 OZ FINELY GRATED CHEDDAR OR PARMESAN CHEESE TO THE PASTRY DOUGH BEFORE ADDING THE WATER.

STILTON & WALNUT TARTLETS

MAKES 12 TARTLETS

Pastry

225 g/8 oz plain flour

pinch of celery salt

100 g/3½ oz cold butter, cut into pieces

25 g/1 oz walnut halves, chopped in a food processor

cold water

Filling

25g/1oz butter

2 celery sticks, trimmed and finely chopped

1 small leek, trimmed and finely chopped

210 ml/7 fl oz double cream, plus 2 tbsp extra

200 g/7 oz Stilton

salt and pepper

3 egg yolks

chopped fresh parsley, to garnish

Lightly butter a 7.5-cm/3-inch, 12-hole muffin tray. Sift the flour and celery salt into a food processor, add the butter and process until the mixture resembles fine breadcrumbs. Tip the mixture into a large bowl and add the walnuts and a little cold water, just enough to bring the dough together. Turn out on to a floured surface and cut the dough in half. Roll out the first piece and cut out 6 × 9-cm/3½-inch circles. Take each circle and roll out to 12 cm/4½ inches diameter and fit into the muffin holes, pressing to fill the holes. Do the same with the remaining dough. Put a piece of baking paper in each hole, fill with baking beans then put the tray in the refrigerator to chill for 30 minutes. Meanwhile, preheat the oven to 200°C/400°F/Gas Mark 6.

Remove the muffin tray from the refrigerator and bake the tartlets blind for 10 minutes in the preheated oven then carefully remove the paper and beans.

Melt the butter in a frying pan and add the celery and leek and cook for 15 minutes, until soft. Add 2 tbsp double cream and crumble in the Stilton, mix well and season with salt and pepper. Bring the remaining cream to simmering point in another pan, then pour on to the egg yolks, stirring all the time. Mix in the Stilton mixture and spoon into the pastry cases. Bake for 10 minutes then turn the tray around in the oven and bake for a further 5 minutes. Cool in the tin for 5 minutes and scatter with parsley.

THIS IS A GOOD PASTRY FOR SAVOURY OR SWEET DISHES. HAZELNUTS AND PECANS ALSO WORK WELL BUT DON'T OVER-CHOP THE NUTS: PULSE IN A FOOD PROCESSOR JUST LONG ENOUGH TO CHOP ROUGHLY BUT FINE ENOUGH TO COMBINE WELL WITH THE PASTRY.

PEA, HAM & CRÈME FRAÎCHE TARTLETS

MAKES 6 TARTLETS

Pastry

125 g/4¹/₂ oz plain flour

pinch of salt

75 g/2¹/₂ oz cold butter, cut into pieces

25 g/1 oz Parmesan cheese, finely grated

cold water

Filling

200 g/7 oz fresh or frozen petits pois

25 g/1 oz unsalted butter

2 shallots, peeled and finely chopped

100 g/3¹/₂ oz cooked ham, chopped

3–4 fresh mint leaves, chopped

120 ml/4 fl oz crème fraîche

3 egg yolks

salt and pepper

Butter 6 x 9-cm/3¹/₂-inch loose-bottomed fluted tart tins. Sift the flour and salt into a food processor, add the butter and process until the mixture resembles fine breadcrumbs. Tip the mixture into a large bowl and add the Parmesan and a little cold water, just enough to bring the dough together. Turn out on to a floured surface and divide into 6 equal-sized pieces. Roll each piece to fit the tart tins. Carefully fit each piece of pastry in its case and press well to fit the tin. Roll the rolling pin over the tin to neaten the

edges and trim the excess pastry. Cut 6 pieces of baking paper and fit a piece into each tart, fill with baking beans and chill in the refrigerator for 30 minutes. Meanwhile, preheat the oven to 200°C/400°F/Gas Mark 6.

Bake the tart cases blind for 10 minutes in the preheated oven then remove the beans and baking paper.

Meanwhile, cook the peas in boiling water for 3–4 minutes, until just tender, then drain. Melt the butter in a frying pan, add the shallots and cook gently for 10 minutes then add the ham and cook for a further 3–5 minutes. Add the peas and chopped mint, remove from the heat and stir in the crème fraîche and egg yolks. Season with salt and pepper and divide among the tart cases. Bake for 12–15 minutes.

FOR A PRETTY ADDITION TO THESE TARTS CRACK A QUAIL'S EGG INTO A SMALL HOLLOW IN THE FILLING OF EACH TART BEFORE BAKING. THESE TARTS HAVE QUITE A DELICATE SUMMERY TASTE AND ARE A PERFECT CHOICE FOR A SUMMER PICNIC OR LUNCH.

ARTICHOKE &
PANCETTA TARTLETS

MAKES 6 TARTLETS

Pastry

125 g/4½ oz plain flour

pinch of salt

75 g/2½ oz cold butter, cut into pieces

cold water

Filling

5 tbsp double cream

4 tbsp bottled artichoke paste

salt and pepper

400 g/14 oz canned artichoke hearts, drained

12 thin-cut pancetta rashers

rocket leaves

50 g/1¾ oz Parmesan or pecorino cheese

2 tbsp olive oil, for drizzling

Butter 6 x 9-cm/3½-inch loose-bottomed fluted tart tins. Sift the flour and salt into a food processor, add the butter and process until the mixture resembles fine breadcrumbs. Tip the mixture into a large bowl and add a little cold water, just enough to bring the dough together. Turn out on to a floured surface and divide into 6 equal-sized pieces. Roll each piece to fit the tart tins. Carefully fit each piece of pastry in its case and press well to fit the tin. Roll the rolling pin over the tin to neaten the edges and trim

the excess pastry. Cut 6 pieces of baking paper and fit a piece into each tart, fill with baking beans and chill in the refrigerator for 30 minutes. Meanwhile, preheat the oven to 200°C/400°F/Gas Mark 6.

Bake the tart cases for 10 minutes in the preheated oven and then remove the beans and baking paper.

Meanwhile, stir the cream and the artichoke paste together and season well with salt and pepper. Divide between the pastry cases, spreading out to cover the base of each tart. Cut each artichoke heart into 3 pieces and divide among the tarts, curl 2 rashers of the pancetta into each tart and bake for 10 minutes. To serve, top each tart with a good amount of rocket then, using a potato peeler, scatter shavings of the Parmesan cheese over the tarts, drizzle with olive oil and serve at once.

OLIVE PASTE (TAPENADE) OR PESTO CAN REPLACE THE ARTICHOKE PASTE; JUST STIR WITH THE CREAM AND SEASON WELL WITH SALT AND PEPPER. FOR A VEGETARIAN VERSION OF THESE TARTS, SUBSTITUTE PEPERONATA (COOKED MIXED PEPPER SLIVERS) OR MOZZARELLA CHEESE FOR THE PANCETTA.

FETA & SPINACH TARTLETS

MAKES 6 TARTLETS

Pastry

125 g/4¹/₂ oz plain flour

pinch of salt

75 g/2¹/₂ oz cold butter, cut into pieces

¹/₂ fresh nutmeg, grated

cold water

Filling

250 g/9 oz baby spinach

25 g/1 oz butter

salt and pepper

150 ml/5 fl oz double cream

3 egg yolks

125 g/4¹/₂ oz feta cheese

50 g/1³/₄ oz pine kernels

Butter 6 x 9-cm/3¹/₂-inch loose-bottomed fluted tart tins. Sift the flour and salt into a food processor, add the butter and process until the mixture resembles fine breadcrumbs. Tip the mixture into a large bowl and add the nutmeg and a little cold water, just enough to bring the dough together. Turn out on to a floured surface and divide into 6 equal-sized pieces. Roll each piece to fit the tart tins. Carefully fit each piece of pastry in its case and press well to fit the tin. Roll the rolling pin over the tin to neaten the edges and trim the excess pastry. Cut 6 pieces of baking paper and fit a piece into each tart, fill with baking beans and chill in the refrigerator for 30 minutes. Meanwhile, preheat the oven to 200°C/400°F/Gas Mark 6.

Bake the tart cases blind for 10 minutes in the preheated oven then remove the beans and paper.

Blanch the spinach in boiling water for just 1 minute then drain, and press to squeeze all the water out. Chop the spinach. Melt the butter in a frying pan, add the spinach and cook gently to evaporate any remaining liquid. Season well with salt and pepper. Stir in the cream and egg yolks. Crumble the feta and divide among the tarts, top with the creamed spinach and bake for 10 minutes. Scatter the pine kernels over the tartlets and cook for a further 5 minutes.

These tarts are delicious hot served with a tomato and olive salad or as part of a Greek supper. They can also be made with filo pastry for an authentic Greek touch.

AUBERGINE, PESTO & PARMA HAM TARTLETS

MAKES 6 TARTLETS

Pastry

175 g/6 oz plain flour

pinch of salt

175 g/6 oz unsalted butter

about 150 ml/5 fl oz chilled water

(or use 250 g/9 oz ready-made puff pastry)

Filling

1 large or 2 small aubergines, trimmed and thinly sliced

5 tbsp olive oil

3 buffalo mozzarella cheeses, sliced

6 tbsp pesto

black pepper

1 egg yolk

6 slices Parma ham

To make the puff pastry sift the flour and salt into a large mixing bowl and rub in 25 g/1 oz butter. Gradually add the water, just enough to bring the dough together, and knead briefly to form a smooth dough. Wrap the dough in clingfilm and chill for 30 minutes. Keep the remaining butter out of the refrigerator and wrap it in a piece of clingfilm then shape it into a 3-cm/1¼-inch thick rectangle. Roll out the dough to a rectangle 3 times longer and 3 cm/1¼ inches wider than the butter and place the butter in the centre, long-side towards you. Fold over the 2 'wings' of pastry to enclose the butter – press down the edges to seal then turn the pastry so the short side faces you. Roll the pastry to its original length, fold into 3, turn and roll again to its original length. Repeat this once more and then rewrap the pastry and chill again for 30 minutes. Remove from the refrigerator and repeat the rolling and turning twice more. Chill again for 30 minutes. At this point you can freeze the pastry until you need it.

When you are ready to make the tarts, cut the pastry into 6 and roll into either circles or rectangles then place on 2 baking trays, 3 on each. Preheat the oven to 190°C/375°F/ Gas Mark 5.

Brush the aubergine slices with 2 tbsp of the olive oil and fry briefly in a non-stick frying pan,

in batches, then arrange the slices neatly overlapping on each pastry base, leaving a 2.5-cm/1-inch margin around the edges. Lay the mozzarella slices over the aubergine slices and spoon over the pesto. Drizzle with the remaining olive oil and season with black pepper. Brush the edges of the pastry with egg yolk and bake for 15 minutes. Remove from the oven and drape a slice of Parma ham on each tart before serving.

HOME-MADE PUFF PASTRY IS NOT DIFFICULT BUT IT IS RATHER TIME-CONSUMING BECAUSE OF ALL THE CHILLING TIME INVOLVED. IF YOU DO HAVE TIME IT REALLY IS WORTH MAKING YOUR OWN, ALTHOUGH READY-MADE PASTRY WILL WORK JUST AS WELL.

Possibly the easiest of tarts to turn out, the savoury main-course tart can be adapted to suit all sorts of occasions. A freeform puff pastry tart taking its inspiration from France or Italy is perfect for a picnic, lunch or supper as it is substantial and satisfying and can be topped with whatever you have in the storecupboard and refrigerator. Bottled or canned Italian vegetables such as peppers, olives and artichokes combined with a little cheese and a few fresh herbs on ready-made puff pastry makes a delicious tart. For something more sophisticated, a crisp pastry shell filled with a creamy fish filling makes an easy, impressive supper dish.

PART TWO
THE ART OF THE TART

MAIN-COURSE
SAVOURY TARTS

Texture and flavour are particularly important when a tart forms the centrepiece of a meal, and a perfectly executed tart can be the most pleasing of dinners as well as a very satisfying dish to produce.

The opportunities to experiment with flavourings for the pastry are considerable and even if you are simply filling your tart with eggs, bacon and cheese, adding a little English mustard powder to the pastry gives an extra dimension. Think around the ingredients and experiment with flavours that complement the filling, but don't be tempted to overdo it, as this should be a subtle addition.

CRAB & WATERCRESS TART

SERVES 6

Pastry

125 g/4¹/₂ oz plain flour

pinch of salt

75 g/2¹/₂ oz cold butter, cut into pieces

cold water

Filling

300 g/10¹/₂ oz prepared white and brown crabmeat

1 bunch watercress, washed and leaves picked from stems

60 ml/2 fl oz milk

2 large eggs, plus 3 egg yolks

210 ml/7 fl oz double cream

salt and pepper

¹/₂ tsp ground nutmeg

¹/₂ bunch fresh chives, snipped

2 tbsp finely grated Parmesan cheese

Lightly butter a 22-cm/9-inch loose-bottomed fluted tart tin. Sift the flour and salt into a food processor, add the butter and process until the mixture resembles fine breadcrumbs. Tip the mixture into a large bowl and add a little cold water, just enough to bring the dough together. Turn out on to a floured surface and roll out the pastry 8 cm/3¹/₄ inches larger than the tin. Carefully lift the pastry into the tin and press to fit. Roll the rolling pin over the tin to neaten the edges and trim the excess pastry. Fit a piece of baking paper into the tart case, fill with baking beans and chill in the refrigerator for 30 minutes. Meanwhile, preheat the oven to 190°C/375°F/Gas Mark 5.

Remove the pastry case from the refrigerator and bake blind for 10 minutes in the preheated oven then remove the beans and paper. Return to the oven for 5 minutes. Remove the tin from the oven and reduce the oven temperature to 160°C/325°F/Gas Mark 3.

Arrange the crabmeat and watercress in the tart tin. Whisk the milk, eggs and egg yolks together in a bowl. Bring the cream to simmering point in a pan and pour over the egg mixture, whisking all the time. Season with salt, pepper and nutmeg and stir in the chives. Carefully pour this mixture over the crab and watercress and scatter over the Parmesan. Bake for 35–40 minutes, until golden and set. Let the tart stand for 10 minutes before serving.

OTHER FISH COULD BE SUBSTITUTED FOR THE CRAB, SUCH AS FLAKED SALMON OR A MIXTURE OF LIGHTLY COOKED WHITE AND SMOKED FISH. YOU COULD ALSO ADD A FEW CAPERS IF YOU LIKE THEM.

TRIPLE TOMATO TART

SERVES 6

Pastry

175 g/6 oz plain flour

pinch of salt

175 g/6 oz unsalted butter

about 150 ml/5 fl oz
chilled water

(or use 250 g/9 oz ready-
made puff pastry)

Topping

3 tbsp sun-dried tomato
purée

250 g/9 oz ripe vine
tomatoes, sliced

150 g/5¹/₂ oz cherry
tomatoes, cut in half

2 sprigs fresh rosemary

2 tbsp extra virgin
olive oil

1 tbsp balsamic vinegar

1 egg yolk

125 g/4¹/₂ oz Italian sliced
salami, chopped

salt and pepper

handful thyme sprigs

To make the puff pastry sift the flour and salt
into a large mixing bowl and rub in 25 g/1 oz
butter. Gradually add the water, just enough to
bring the pastry together, and knead briefly to
form a smooth dough. Wrap the dough in
clingfilm and chill for 30 minutes. Keep the
remaining butter out of the refrigerator, wrap it
in a piece of clingfilm and shape it into a 3-cm/
1¹/₄-inch thick rectangle. Roll out the dough to a
rectangle 3 times longer and 3 cm/1¹/₄ inches
wider than the butter and place the butter in
the centre, long-side towards you. Fold over the
2 'wings' of pastry to enclose the butter – press
down the edges to seal and then turn the pastry
so the short side faces you. Roll the pastry to its
original length, fold into 3, turn and roll again to
its original length. Repeat this once more and
then rewrap the pastry and chill again for
30 minutes. Remove from the refrigerator and
repeat the rolling and turning twice more. Chill
again for 30 minutes. At this point you can
freeze the pastry until you need it.

You can use any combination of tomatoes
here, including a few strips of sun-dried
tomatoes in oil when you add the salami. A
mixture of yellow and red tomatoes looks
pretty, or use roasted peppers and pine kernels
instead of the salami, and add a few slices of
soft goat's cheese before baking.

When you are ready to make your tart,
preheat the oven to 190°C/375°F/Gas Mark 5.
Roll out the pastry to form a rectangle 36 cm/
14 inches long and 25 cm/10 inches wide and lift
on to a heavy-duty baking tray. Spread the sun-
dried tomato purée over the pastry leaving a
3 cm/1¹/₄-inch margin around the edge. Arrange
the vine tomato slices over the tomato purée,
scatter over the cherry tomato halves, top with
the rosemary and drizzle with 1 tbsp olive oil
and the balsamic vinegar. Brush the edges of
the pastry with the egg yolk and bake for
10 minutes. Scatter over the salami and bake
for a further 10–15 minutes.

Remove the tart from the oven and season
with salt and pepper. Drizzle with the remaining
oil and scatter over the thyme.

POTATO, FONTINA & ROSEMARY TART

SERVES 6

Pastry

175 g/6 oz plain flour

pinch of salt

175 g/6 oz unsalted butter

about 150 ml/5 fl oz chilled water

(or use 250 g/9 oz ready-made puff pastry)

Filling

3–4 medium waxy potatoes

300 g/10½ oz fontina cheese, cut into cubes

1 red onion, sliced thinly

3 large sprigs fresh rosemary

2 tbsp olive oil

salt and pepper

1 egg yolk

To make the puff pastry sift the flour and salt into a large mixing bowl and rub in 25 g/1 oz butter. Gradually add the water, just enough to bring the pastry together, and knead briefly to form a smooth dough. Wrap the dough in clingfilm and chill for 30 minutes. Keep the remaining butter out of the refrigerator, wrap it in a piece of clingfilm and shape it into a 3-cm/1¼-inches thick rectangle. Roll out the dough to a rectangle 3 times longer and 3 cm/1¼ inches wider than the butter and place the butter in the centre, long-side towards you. Fold over the 2 'wings' of pastry to enclose the butter – press down the edges to seal and then turn the pastry so the short side faces you. Roll the pastry to its original length, fold into 3, turn and roll again to its original length. Repeat this once more then rewrap the pastry and chill again for 30 minutes. Remove from the refrigerator and repeat the rolling and turning twice more. Chill again for 30 minutes. At this point you can freeze the pastry until you need it.

Roll the pastry into a large circle and place on a baking tray. Preheat the oven to 190°C/375°F/ Gas Mark 5. Peel the potatoes and slice them as thinly as possible, so they are almost transparent – a mandolin is the best utensil for this, if you have one. Arrange the potato slices in a spiral, overlapping the slices to cover the pastry and

leaving a 2-cm/¾-inch margin around the edge. Arrange the cheese and onion over the potatoes, scatter with the rosemary and drizzle over the olive oil. Season with salt and pepper and brush the edges with the egg yolk. Bake for 25 minutes, until the potatoes are tender and the pastry brown and crisp.

YOU CAN USE DIFFERENT CHEESES IN THIS TART – GORGONZOLA WORKS WELL – AND ADD A FEW LARDONS OR BACON PIECES. OREGANO CAN REPLACE THE ROSEMARY. AND YOU CAN ADD A HANDFUL OF STONED BLACK OLIVES IF YOU WISH.

SQUASH, SAGE & GORGONZOLA TART

SERVES 6

Pastry

125 g/4¹/₂ oz plain flour

pinch of salt

75 g/2¹/₂ oz cold butter, cut into pieces

cold water

Filling

¹/₂ small butternut squash or 1 slice pumpkin, weighing 250 g/9 oz

1 tsp olive oil

270 ml/9 fl oz double cream

salt and pepper

175 g/6 oz Gorgonzola cheese

2 eggs, plus 1 egg yolk

6–8 fresh sage leaves

Cut the squash in half and brush the cut side with the oil. Place cut-side up on a baking tray and bake for 30–40 minutes, until browned and very soft. Leave to cool. Remove the seeds and scoop out the flesh into a large bowl, discarding the skin.

Lightly butter a 22-cm/9-inch loose-bottomed fluted tart tin. Sift the flour and salt into a food processor, add the butter and process until the mixture resembles fine breadcrumbs. Tip the mixture into a large bowl and add a little cold water, just enough to bring the dough together. Turn out on to a floured surface and roll out the pastry 8 cm/3¹/₄ inches larger than the tin. Carefully lift the pastry into the tin and press to fit. Roll the rolling pin over the tin to neaten the edges and remove the excess pastry from the edges. Fit a piece of baking paper into the tart case, fill with baking beans and chill in the refrigerator for 30 minutes. Meanwhile, preheat the oven to 190°C/375°F/Gas Mark 5.

Remove the pastry case from the refrigerator and bake the tart case blind for 10 minutes in the preheated oven then remove the beans and paper. Return to the oven for 5 minutes.

Mash the squash and mix with half the cream, season with salt and pepper and spread in the pastry case. Slice the cheese and lay it on top. Whisk the remaining cream with the eggs and egg yolk and pour the mixture into the tart tin, making sure it settles evenly. Arrange the sage leaves in a circle on the surface. Bake for 30–35 minutes and leave for 10 minutes in the tin before serving.

THIS TART IS BEST EATEN WARM. THE SQUASH GIVES IT A SLIGHT SWEETNESS, WHICH COMPLEMENTS THE CHEESE PERFECTLY AND MAKES IT POPULAR WITH CHILDREN.

YELLOW
COURGETTE TART

SERVES 6

Pastry

250 g/9 oz plain flour

pinch of salt

125 g/4¹/₂ oz cold butter, cut into pieces

50 g/1³/₄ oz Parmesan cheese, grated

1 egg

cold water

Filling

2 large yellow courgettes

1 tbsp salt

50 g/1³/₄ oz unsalted butter

1 bunch spring onions, trimmed and finely sliced

150 ml/5 fl oz double cream

3 large eggs

salt and white pepper

1 small bunch fresh chives, chopped

Butter a 25-cm/10-inch loose-bottomed tart tin. Sift the flour and salt into a food processor, add the butter and pulse to combine, then tip into a large bowl. Add the Parmesan cheese and mix together the egg and water. Add most of the egg mixture and work to a soft dough, using more egg mixture if needed. Turn out on to a floured surface and roll out the pastry 8 cm/3¹/₄ inches larger than the tin. Carefully lift the pastry into the tin and press to fit. Roll the rolling pin over the tin to neaten the edges and trim the excess pastry. Fit a piece of baking paper into the tart case, fill with baking beans and chill in the refrigerator for 30 minutes. Meanwhile, preheat the oven to 200°C/400°F/ Gas Mark 6.

Bake the tart case blind for 15 minutes in the preheated oven then remove the beans and paper and bake for a further 5 minutes. Remove from the oven and cool. Reduce the oven temperature to 180°C/350°F/Gas Mark 4.

Meanwhile, grate the courgettes and put in a colander with 1 tbsp salt. Leave to drain for 20 minutes then rinse and put in a clean tea towel, squeezing all the moisture from the courgettes. Keep dry.

Melt the butter in a wide frying pan, sauté the spring onions until soft then add the courgettes and cook over a medium heat for 5 minutes, until any liquid has evaporated. Cool slightly. Whisk the cream and eggs together with the salt and pepper and chives. Spoon the courgettes into the tart case and pour in the cream mixture, making sure it settles properly, and bake for 30 minutes. Serve hot or cold.

SPRING VEGETABLE TART

SERVES 6

Pastry

250 g/9 oz plain flour

pinch of salt

125 g/4¹/₂ oz cold butter, cut into pieces

50 g/1³/₄ oz grated Parmesan cheese

1 egg

cold water

Filling

300 g/11 oz selection of baby spring vegetables, such as carrots, asparagus, peas, broad beans, salad onions, corn cobs, leeks

300 ml/11 fl oz double cream

125 g/4¹/₂ oz mature Cheddar cheese, grated

2 eggs plus 3 egg yolks

salt and pepper

handful tarragon and flat-leaved parsley, chopped

USE ONLY THE MOST TENDER OF YOUNG VEGETABLES FOR THIS TART. IF THEY ARE REALLY SMALL, YOU CAN LEAVE THEM WHOLE. A FEW SLICES OF SOFT GOAT'S CHEESE COULD BE ADDED JUST BEFORE BAKING.

Butter a 25-cm/10-inch loose-bottomed tart tin. Sift the flour and salt into a food processor, add the butter and pulse to combine, then tip into a large bowl and add the Parmesan cheese. Mix the egg and water together in a small bowl. Add most of the egg mixture and work into a soft dough, using more egg mixture if needed. Turn out on to a floured surface and roll out the pastry 8 cm/3¹/₄ inches larger than the tin. Carefully lift the pastry into the tin and press to fit. Roll the rolling pin over the tin to neaten the edges and trim the excess pastry. Fit a piece of baking paper into the tart case, fill with baking beans and chill in the refrigerator for 30 minutes. Meanwhile, preheat the oven to 200°C/400°F/Gas Mark 6.

Bake the tart case blind for 15 minutes in the preheated oven then remove the beans and paper and bake for a further 5 minutes. Remove from the oven and cool. Reduce the oven temperature to 180°C/350°F/Gas Mark 4.

Prepare the vegetables by trimming and peeling where necessary, then cut them into bite-sized pieces and blanch in boiling water. Drain and cool. Bring the cream to simmering point in a pan. Place the cheese, eggs and egg yolks in a heatproof bowl and pour the warm cream over the mixture. Stir to combine, season well with salt and pepper and stir in the herbs. Arrange the vegetables in the tart case, pour over the cheese custard and bake for 30–40 minutes, until just set. Cool in the tin for 10 minutes before serving.

CURRIED ONION TART

SERVES 6

Pastry

125 g/4¹/₂ oz plain flour

pinch of salt

75 g/2¹/₂ oz cold butter, cut into pieces

¹/₂ tsp ground cumin

cold water

Filling

1 tsp vegetable oil

25 g/1 oz butter

1 tsp garam masala

1 tsp ground coriander

1 tsp turmeric

¹/₂ tsp ground cumin

¹/₂ tsp ground ginger

1 garlic clove, crushed

500 g/1 lb 2 oz onions, thinly sliced

1 tsp brown sugar

2 eggs, plus 2 egg yolks

270 ml/9 fl oz double cream

salt and pepper

bunch fresh coriander, chopped

Lightly butter a 22-cm/9-inch loose-bottomed fluted tart tin. Sift the flour and salt into a food processor, add the butter and process until the mixture resembles fine breadcrumbs. Tip the mixture into a large bowl, sprinkle in the cumin and a little cold water, just enough to bring the dough together. Turn out on to a floured surface and roll out the pastry 8 cm/3¹/₄ inches larger than the tin. Carefully lift the pastry into the tin and press to fit. Roll the rolling pin over the tin to neaten the edges and trim the excess pastry. Fit a piece of baking paper into the tart case, fill with baking beans and chill for 30 minutes. Meanwhile, preheat the oven to 190°C/375°F/ Gas Mark 5.

Remove the pastry case from the refrigerator and bake the tart case blind for 10 minutes in the preheated oven then remove the beans and baking paper. Return to the oven for 5 minutes.

Meanwhile, heat the oil and butter in a frying pan, stir in the spices and cook for 2 minutes. Add the garlic, onion and sugar and cook for 10 minutes then cover the pan and cook for a

further 20 minutes, until the onion is very soft. Remove the lid and let the onions colour and caramelize slightly. Beat the eggs, egg yolks and cream together and season with salt and pepper. Spoon the onions into the tart case and pour in the eggs and cream. Scatter some fresh coriander over the top and bake for 30–35 minutes. Cool in the tin for 10 minutes then scatter over more coriander before serving.

THIS TART, WITH ITS INDIAN FLAVOURS, IS GOOD SERVED WITH A COOLING CUCUMBER RAITA: STIR A LITTLE CHOPPED CUCUMBER INTO NATURAL YOGURT, ADD A LITTLE SALT AND SCATTER OVER A FEW TOASTED FLAKED ALMONDS. THIS RECIPE ALSO WORKS WELL FOR INDIVIDUAL TARTLETS, TOPPED WITH A LITTLE MANGO CHUTNEY BEFORE SERVING.

SMOKED HADDOCK & GRUYERE SOUFFLE TART

SERVES 6

Pastry

125 g/4¹/₂ oz plain flour

pinch of salt

75 g/2¹/₂ oz cold butter,
cut into pieces

¹/₂ tsp English mustard
powder

I egg yolk

cold water

Filling

250 g/9 oz undyed
smoked haddock

300 ml/10 fl oz milk

I bay leaf

25 g/I oz butter

25 g/I oz plain flour

¹/₂ tsp ground nutmeg

white pepper

125 g/4¹/₂ oz Gruyère
cheese, grated

2 eggs, separated

Lightly butter a 22-cm/9-inch loose-bottomed fluted tart tin. Sift the flour and salt into a food processor, add the butter and process until the mixture resembles fine breadcrumbs. Tip the mixture into a large bowl and sprinkle in the mustard powder. Mix the egg yolk with a little cold water and add a little of the mixture to the bowl, just enough bring the dough together. Turn out on to a floured surface and roll out the pastry 8 cm/3¹/₄ inches larger than the tin. Carefully lift the pastry into the tin and press to fit. Roll the rolling pin over the tin to neaten the edges and trim the excess pastry. Fit a piece of baking paper into the tart case, fill with baking beans and chill in the refrigerator for 30 minutes. Meanwhile, preheat the oven to 190°C/375°F/Gas Mark 5.

Remove the pastry case from the refrigerator and bake the tart case blind for 10 minutes in the preheated oven then remove the beans and baking paper. Return to the oven for 5 minutes.

Meanwhile, put the haddock, milk and bay leaf in a shallow frying pan, bring to simmering point

and poach the fish for 3–5 minutes, until just cooked. Remove from the heat, discard the bay leaf and carefully lift out the fish, reserving the milk. Cool the fish slightly and flake, discarding any bones or skin. Increase the oven temperature to 200°C/400°F/Gas Mark 6.

Melt the butter in a medium saucepan and stir in the flour to make a roux. Gradually add the reserved cooking milk, stirring well to combine, and cook for 5 minutes until thickened. Stir in the nutmeg and pepper and then the cheese. Remove the sauce from the heat, stir in the egg yolks and fish and allow to cool slightly. Meanwhile, whisk the egg whites until stiff then fold quickly and lightly into the fish mixture. Immediately pour into the tart case and bake for 15 minutes, until puffed up and browned. Remove the tart from the oven and allow to rest for 10 minutes before serving.

THIS IMPRESSIVE LOOKING TART CAN BE MADE SIMPLY WITH CHEESE, INSTEAD OF THE HADDOCK. USE A COMBINATION OF YOUR FAVOURITE CHEESES OR USE A LITTLE CHOPPED COOKED HAM AND SOME SOFT HERBS INSTEAD OF THE FISH.

GOAT'S CHEESE
& THYME TART

SERVES 6

Pastry

175 g/6 oz plain flour

pinch of salt

175 g/6 oz unsalted butter

about 150 ml/5 fl oz
chilled water

(or use 250 g/9 oz
ready-made puff pastry)

Topping

500 g/1 lb 2 oz goat's
cheese, such as chèvre,
sliced

3–4 sprigs fresh thyme,
leaves picked from stalks

50 g/1³/₄ oz black olives,
stoned

1 x 50 g/1³/₄ oz anchovies
in olive oil

1 tbsp olive oil

salt and black pepper

1 egg yolk

To make the puff pastry sift the flour and salt into a large mixing bowl and rub in 25 g/1 oz butter. Gradually add the water, just enough to bring the pastry together, and knead briefly to form a smooth dough. Wrap the dough in clingfilm and chill for 30 minutes. Keep the remaining butter out of the refrigerator, wrap it in a piece of clingfilm and shape it into a 3-cm/1¹/₄-inches thick rectangle. Roll out the dough to a rectangle 3 times longer and 3 cm/1¹/₄ inches

wider than the butter and place the butter in the centre, long-side towards you. Fold over the 2 'wings' of pastry to enclose the butter – press down the edges to seal and then turn the pastry so the short side faces you. Roll the pastry to its original length, fold into 3, turn and roll again to its original length. Repeat this once more and then rewrap the pastry and chill again for 30 minutes. Remove from the refrigerator and repeat the rolling and turning twice more, chilling again for 30 minutes. At this point you can freeze the pastry until you need it.

Roll the pastry into a large circle or rectangle and place on a baking tray. Preheat the oven to 190°C/375°F/Gas Mark 5.

Arrange the cheese slices on the pastry, leaving a 2.5-cm/1-inch margin around the edge. Sprinkle the thyme and olives, and arrange the anchovy fillets, over the cheese. Drizzle over the olive oil. Season well and brush the edges of the pastry with the egg. Bake for 20–25 minutes, until the cheese is bubbling and the pastry is browned.

SERVE THIS TART HOT, STRAIGHT FROM THE OVEN, AND SCATTER OVER A FEW ROCKET LEAVES OR SHREDDED RADICCHIO, DRIZZLE WITH OLIVE OIL AND SPRINKLE A FEW CHOPPED WALNUTS OVER THE TOP.

There are an infinite number of possibilities with fruit tarts. The fruit specified in the recipe can almost always be substituted for your own favourite fruit. For autumn and winter, fruits such as apples lend themselves to delicious treatments such as Tarte Tatin. Pears work particularly well with more robust pastry and comforting accompaniments such as custard or crème anglaise. Summer fruit tarts with crisp buttery pastry and soft fruits are a wonderful treat and can be made into a dramatic centrepiece for a summer lunch or dinner, while tropical fruits look beautiful and taste delightfully sweet.

As we now have a broader choice of exotic fruits, the possibilities for creative tart-making are endless. Experiment with lesser-known fruit such as quince, which has a unique fragrance and flavour and can often be used where apples and pears are specified. Pastry with a hint of cinnamon or nutmeg works very well with

PART THREE FRUITFUL
SUMPTUOUS FRUIT TARTS

traditional English fruits, and pastries such as almond or coconut are ideal for tropical tarts.

The easiest of tarts is a pastry case baked blind then filled with sweetened whipped cream and topped with berries or poached fruits. Take into account colour contrasts in presenting these tarts – the velvety purple of blueberries looks wonderful with the bright orange of mango or papaya, and the jewel-like colours of redcurrants or pomegranate seeds are perfectly set off against cream-filled chocolate pastry.

BRAMBLE TART WITH CASSIS CREAM

SERVES 6

Pastry

350 g/12 oz plain flour

pinch of salt

175 g/6 oz unsalted butter

50 g/1³/₄ oz caster sugar

cold water

Filling

750 g/1 lb 10 oz
blackberries

6 tbsp golden caster sugar

1 tbsp cassis

5 tsp semolina

1 egg white

To serve

270 ml/9 fl oz double
cream

1 tbsp cassis

fresh mint leaves

To make the pastry sift the flour and salt into a large bowl and rub in the butter. Stir in the sugar and add enough cold water to bring the dough together, then wrap in clingfilm and chill for 30 minutes.

Meanwhile, rinse and pick over the blackberries then put in a bowl with 4 tbsp of the sugar and cassis, stirring to coat. Preheat the oven to 200°C/400°F/Gas Mark 6.

Roll out the pastry to a large circle, handling carefully because it is quite a soft dough. Leave the edges ragged and place on a baking tray. Sprinkle the pastry with the semolina, leaving a good 6-cm/2¹/₂-inch edge. Pile the fruit into the middle and brush the edges of the pastry with the egg white. Fold in the edges of the pastry to overlap and enclose the fruit, making sure to press together the pastry in order to close any gaps. Brush with the remaining egg white, sprinkle with the remaining sugar and bake for 25 minutes.

To serve, whip the cream until it begins to thicken and stir in the cassis. Serve the tart hot, straight from the oven, with a good dollop of the cassis cream and garnished with mint leaves.

THIS CAN ALSO BE MADE WITH A MIXTURE OF BERRIES: MIX SOME RASPBERRIES, STRAWBERRIES OR SLICES OF RIPE PLUM OR PEACH IN WITH THE BLACKBERRIES. USE CASSIS OR A NON-ALCOHOLIC BLACKBERRY-FLAVOURED CORDIAL. ALSO GOOD SERVED WITH ICE CREAM.

TOFFEE APPLE TART

SERVES 6

Pastry

125 g/4¹/₂ oz plain flour

pinch of salt

75 g/2¹/₂ oz cold butter, cut into pieces

cold water

Filling

1.3 kg/3 lb Cox's Orange Pippin or other firm, sweet apples, peeled and cored

1 tsp lemon juice

50 g/1³/₄ oz butter

100 g/3¹/₂ oz caster sugar

200 g/7 oz granulated sugar

90 ml/3 fl oz cold water

150 ml/5 fl oz double cream

icing sugar, to dust

Lightly butter a 22-cm/9-inch loose-bottomed fluted tart tin. Sift the flour and salt into a food processor, add the butter and process until the mixture resembles fine breadcrumbs. Tip the mixture into a large bowl and add the cold water to bring the dough together. Turn out on to a floured surface and roll out the pastry 8 cm/3¹/₄ inches larger than the tin. Carefully lift the pastry into the tin and press to fit. Roll the rolling pin over the tin to neaten the edges and trim the excess pastry. Fit a piece of baking paper into the tart case, fill with baking beans and chill in the refrigerator for 30 minutes. Meanwhile, preheat the oven to 190°C/375°F/Gas Mark 5.

Remove the pastry case from the refrigerator and bake blind for 10 minutes in the preheated oven then remove the beans and paper. Return to the oven for 5 minutes.

Meanwhile, take 4 apples, cut each one into 8 pieces and toss in the lemon juice. Melt the butter in a frying pan and sauté the apple pieces until just beginning to caramelize and brown on the edges. Remove from the pan and cool.

Slice the remaining apples thinly, put them in a saucepan with the caster sugar and cook for about 20–30 minutes, until soft. Spoon the cooked, sliced apple into the pastry case and arrange the reserved apple pieces on top in a circle. Bake for 30 minutes.

Put the granulated sugar and water in a saucepan and heat until the sugar dissolves. Boil to form a caramel. Remove from the heat and add the cream, stirring constantly to combine into toffee. Remove the tart from the oven, pour the toffee over the apples and chill for 1 hour. When ready to serve sift a little icing sugar over the tart. Serve with thick cream.

THIS TART WOULD ALSO WORK WELL WITH OTHER FRUIT, SUCH AS PEARS OR QUINCES, OR AS INDIVIDUAL TARTLETS, EACH ONE CONTAINING AN APRICOT OR A FEW APPLE SLICES SMOTHERED IN THE TOFFEE SAUCE.

LEMON GRASS & MANGO TART

SERVES 6

Coconut Pastry

225 g/8 oz plain flour

pinch of salt

125 g/4¹/₂ oz cold butter, cut into pieces

50 g/1³/₄ oz desiccated coconut

1 tbsp icing sugar

cold water

Filling

3 lemon grass stalks

390 ml/13 fl oz double cream

4 egg yolks

100 g/3¹/₂ oz golden caster sugar

2 pieces or 6 g/¹/₄ oz fine leaf gelatine

1 large ripe mango or 2 small Alphonso mangoes

1–2 tsp icing sugar

Finely chop the lemon grass into small pieces or finely grind in a food processor, put in a saucepan with the cream and bring to the boil. Remove from the heat, cover and leave to infuse for 1 hour.

Lightly butter a 22-cm/9-inch loose-bottomed fluted tart tin. Sift the flour and salt into a food processor, add the butter and process until the mixture resembles fine breadcrumbs. Tip the mixture into a large bowl, stir in the coconut and sugar and add a little cold water, just enough

THIS TART CAN BE SERVED AS A SIMPLE UNCARAMELIZED LEMON GRASS TART, WITHOUT THE MANGO, OR YOU CAN SUBSTITUTE OTHER EXOTIC FRUITS OR BERRIES. ANOTHER OPTION IS TO DISPENSE WITH THE FRUIT AND BRÛLÉ THE TOP INSTEAD.

to bring the dough together. Turn out on to a floured surface and roll out the pastry 8 cm/3¹/₄ inches larger than the tin. Carefully lift the pastry into the tin and press to fit. Roll the rolling pin over the tin to neaten the edges and trim the excess pastry. Fit a piece of baking paper into the tart case, fill with baking beans and chill in the refrigerator for 30 minutes. Meanwhile, preheat the oven to 190°C/375°F/Gas Mark 5.

Remove the pastry case from the refrigerator and bake blind for 15 minutes in the preheated oven then remove the beans and paper. Return to the oven for 10 minutes then remove and leave to cool completely.

Whisk together the egg yolks and sugar. Strain the cream into a clean saucepan to remove the lemon grass and whisk in the eggs and sugar. Place on a low heat and cook until slightly thickened. Meanwhile, soften the gelatine in a little cold water for 2–3 minutes then lift out of the water and stir into the hot cream. When the gelatine has dissolved remove the pan from the heat and cool. Pour the cream mixture into the cold tart case and chill for 3–4 hours. When you are ready to serve, peel, stone and thinly slice the mango and arrange randomly over the lemon grass custard to cover the surface. Sprinkle with the icing sugar and caramelize with a blowtorch.

PEACH & STEM GINGER TARTE TATIN

SERVES 6

Pastry

175 g/6 oz plain flour

pinch of salt

175 g/6 oz unsalted butter

about 150 ml/5 fl oz chilled water

(or use 250 g/9 oz ready-made puff pastry)

Filling

6–8 just ripe peaches

75 g/3 oz golden caster sugar

50 g/1¾ oz unsalted butter

3 pieces stem ginger in syrup, chopped

1 tbsp ginger syrup from the stem ginger jar

1 egg, beaten

To make the puff pastry sift the flour and salt into a large mixing bowl and rub in 25 g/1 oz butter. Gradually add the water, just enough to bring the pastry together, and knead briefly to form a smooth dough. Wrap the dough in clingfilm and chill for 30 minutes. Keep the remaining butter out of the refrigerator, wrap it in a piece of clingfilm and shape it into a 3-cm/1¼-inches thick rectangle. Roll out the dough to a rectangle 3 times longer and 3 cm/1¼ inches wider than the butter and place the butter in the centre, long-side towards you. Fold over the 2 'wings' of pastry to enclose the butter – press down the edges to seal and then turn the pastry so the short side faces you. Roll the pastry to its original length, fold into 3, turn and roll again to its original length. Repeat this once more then rewrap the pastry and chill again for 30 minutes. Remove from the refrigerator and repeat the rolling and turning twice more then chill again for 30 minutes. At this point you can freeze the pastry until you need it.

Preheat the oven to 190°C/375°F/Gas Mark 5. Plunge the peaches into boiling water then drain and peel. Cut each in half. Put the sugar in a 25-cm/10-inch heavy, ovenproof frying pan and heat it gently until it caramelizes. Don't stir, just shake the pan if necessary. Once the sugar turns a dark caramel colour, remove from the heat and drop 25 g/1 oz of the butter into it.

Place the peaches cut-side up on top of the caramel, packing them as close together as possible and tucking the stem ginger pieces into any gaps. Dot with the remaining butter and drizzle with the ginger syrup. Return to a gentle heat while you roll out the pastry in a circle larger than the pan you are using. Drape the pastry over the peaches and tuck it in well around the edges, brush with the beaten egg and bake for 20–25 minutes, until the pastry is browned and puffed up. Remove from the oven and leave to rest for 5 minutes then invert on to a serving plate and serve with thick cream or ice cream.

THIS IS A MODERN TAKE ON THE TRADITIONAL APPLE TARTE TATIN. YOU CAN USE OTHER FRUITS – PLUMS, APPLES AND PEARS ALL WORK WELL. PUFF PASTRY IS PARTICULARLY DELICIOUS BUT SHORTCRUST OR FILO COULD ALSO BE USED.

LEMON CURD
& BLUEBERRY TART

SERVES 6

Pastry

175 g/6 oz plain flour

1 tsp icing sugar

pinch of salt

100 g/3 1/2 oz cold butter,
cut into pieces

1 egg yolk

finely grated rind of
1/2 lemon

cold water

Filling

2 large eggs

75 g/3 oz caster sugar

100 g/3 1/2 oz unsalted
butter, cut into cubes

juice of 2–3 lemons
(120 ml/4 fl oz)

350 g/12 oz fresh
blueberries

1 tbsp cassis (optional)

1 tbsp icing sugar
(optional)

To decorate

finely grated rind of the
lemons used in the filling

icing sugar

This tart looks very pretty made in a fluted
loose-bottomed rectangular tart tin, 33 x 10 cm/
13 x 4 inches wide, or a 22-cm/9-inch round tin.
Make the lemon curd filling first. Put the eggs in
a heatproof bowl and whisk in the sugar. Add
the cubed butter and the lemon juice and place
over a saucepan of simmering water, whisking
constantly until the ingredients are well
combined. Continue stirring for 10 minutes, until
the mixture thickens. Remove from the heat and
leave to cool. Keep covered until needed.

To make the pastry put the flour, sugar
and salt in a food processor, add the butter
and process until the mixture resembles
breadcrumbs. Tip into a large bowl, add the
egg yolk and lemon rind and bring the pastry

together, adding a little cold water if necessary.
Turn out on to a floured surface and roll out to
8 cm/3 1/4 inches larger than the tin. Carefully lift
the pastry into the tin and press to fit. Roll the
rolling pin over the tin to neaten the edges
and trim the excess pastry. Fit a piece of
baking paper into the tart case, fill with
baking beans and chill in the refrigerator for
30 minutes. Meanwhile, preheat the oven to
190°C/375°F/Gas Mark 5.

Remove the pastry case from the refrigerator
and bake the tart case blind for 15 minutes in
the preheated oven then remove the beans
and paper. Return to the oven for 10 minutes
then remove and cool completely. Spoon the
lemon curd into the tart shell and top with
the blueberries. (If you wish, you can poach the
blueberries with the cassis and sugar until glossy.
Just before the berries start to burst, cool
completely and spoon over the curd). Top with
the finely grated lemon rind and a little sifted
icing sugar.

TO MAKE ORANGE CURD, SUBSTITUTE
ORANGE JUICE AND GRATED ORANGE
RIND FOR THE LEMON JUICE AND
RIND. SPREAD OVER THE TART SHELL
AND TOP WITH PEELED ORANGE SLICES
DRIZZLED WITH A LITTLE ORANGE
FLOWER WATER.

JEWEL BERRY TART

SERVES 6

Pastry

125 g/4¹/2 oz plain flour

2 tsp cocoa powder

2 tsp icing sugar

pinch of salt

75 g/2¹/2 oz cold butter, cut into pieces

1 egg yolk

ice-cold water

Filling

¹/2 punnet each blackcurrants, redcurrants and white currants

seeds of 1 large pomegranate

6 egg yolks

75 g/2¹/2 oz caster sugar

600 ml/1 pint double cream

1 vanilla pod, split and the seeds scraped out

Lightly butter a 22-cm/9-inch loose-bottomed fluted tart tin. Sift the flour, cocoa powder, icing sugar and salt into a food processor, add the butter and process until the mixture resembles fine breadcrumbs. Tip the mixture into a large bowl and add the egg yolk plus a little ice-cold water to bring the dough together. Turn out on to a surface dusted with more flour and cocoa powder and roll out the pastry 8 cm/3¹/4 inches larger than the tin. Carefully lift the pastry into the tin and press to fit. Roll the rolling pin over the tin to neaten the edges and trim the excess pastry. Fit a piece of baking paper into the tart case, fill with baking beans and chill in the refrigerator for 30 minutes. Meanwhile, preheat the oven to 190°C/375°F/Gas Mark 5.

Remove the pastry case from the refrigerator and bake the pastry blind for 15 minutes in the preheated oven then remove the beans and paper. Return to the oven for 10 minutes then remove and cool. Run the prongs of a fork along the currant stalks to pick off the currants and mix with the pomegranate seeds. Chill.

You can add a little icing sugar and pomegranate molasses or cassis to the fruits before topping the tart and sift a little icing sugar over the berries before serving.

Whisk the egg yolks with the sugar in a heatproof bowl and place over a saucepan of simmering water, whisking for 10 minutes, or until the mixture has thickened. In a separate saucepan bring the double cream and the split vanilla pod to the boil then whisk into the eggs and sugar. Stir constantly for a further 5–8 minutes.

Take the custard off the heat and remove the vanilla pod. (The pod can be wiped dry and re-used in another recipe). Leave to cool completely then pour into the tart case and chill for 3–4 hours. When you are ready to serve, pile the jewelled berries over the set custard.

STRAWBERRY & ELDERFLOWER TART

SERVES 6

Pastry

175 g/6 oz plain flour

pinch of salt

100 g/3¹/₂ oz cold butter, cut into pieces

1 tsp icing sugar

1 egg yolk

cold water

Filling

120 ml/4 fl oz elderflower cordial

50 ml/2 fl oz rosé or white wine

500 g/1 lb 2 oz strawberries, hulled

275 ml/10 fl oz double cream

¹/₂ tsp vanilla extract

2 tbsp icing sugar

This tart looks very pretty made in a fluted loose-bottomed rectangular tart tin, 36 × 13 cm/14 × 5 inches, or a 22-cm/9-inch loose-bottomed fluted tart tin. Sift the flour and salt into a food processor, add the butter and process until the mixture resembles fine breadcrumbs. Tip the mixture into a large bowl, stir in the sugar, and add the egg yolk and a little cold water to bring the dough together. Turn out on to a floured surface and roll out the pastry 8 cm/3¹/₄ inches larger than the tin. Carefully lift the pastry into the tin and press to fit. Roll the rolling pin over the tin to neaten the edges and trim the excess pastry. Fit a piece of baking paper into the tart case, fill with baking beans and chill in the refrigerator for 30 minutes. Meanwhile, preheat the oven to 190°C/375°F/ Gas Mark 5.

Remove the pastry case from the refrigerator and bake the tart case blind for 20 minutes in the preheated oven then remove the beans and paper. Return to the oven for 10 minutes then remove and cool completely.

A LITTLE ICING SUGAR SIFTED OVER THE TART JUST BEFORE SERVING ADDS AN ATTRACTIVE FINISH. IF THERE ISN'T ENOUGH SYRUP LEFT FOR DRIZZLING, MIX WHAT YOU HAVE WITH A LITTLE EXTRA WINE AND SUGAR.

Bring the cordial and wine to the boil in a small saucepan and simmer for 5 minutes then cool completely. Cut the strawberries into 1-cm/¹/₂-inch slices, place in a bowl and pour over the elderflower syrup. Chill until needed. Remove the pastry case carefully from its tin and transfer to a serving plate.

Put the cream in a bowl and whisk until starting to thicken, add the vanilla and sugar and whisk again until thick. Spoon into the tart case and chill for 30 minutes. Lift the strawberries from the syrup and arrange them randomly or in a fish-scale pattern over the cream. Serve the elderflower syrup in a small jug for drizzling over the tart.

PASSION FRUIT BRULÉE TART

SERVES 6

Pastry

125 g/4¹/₂ oz plain flour

pinch of salt

75 g/3 oz cold butter, cut into pieces

1 tsp icing sugar

cold water

Filling

6 egg yolks

75 g/3 oz caster sugar

600 ml/1 pint double cream

4 passion fruit

4 tbsp icing sugar

Lightly butter a 22-cm/9-inch loose-bottomed fluted tart tin. Sift the flour and salt into a food processor, add the butter and process until the mixture resembles fine breadcrumbs. Tip the mixture into a large bowl, stir in the sugar and add a little cold water, just enough to bring the dough together. Turn out on to a floured surface and roll out the pastry 8 cm/3¹/₄ inches larger than the tin. Carefully lift the pastry into the tin and press to fit. Roll the rolling pin over the tin to neaten the edges and trim the excess pastry. Fit a piece of baking paper into the tart case, fill with baking beans and chill for 30 minutes. Meanwhile, preheat the oven to 190°C/375°F/Gas Mark 5.

Remove the pastry case from the refrigerator and bake blind for 20 minutes in the preheated oven then remove the beans and paper. Return to the oven for 10 minutes then remove and cool completely.

Whisk the egg yolks with the caster sugar in a heatproof bowl and place over a saucepan of

simmering water, continuing to whisk for 10 minutes, until the mixture has thickened. In a separate saucepan bring the double cream to the boil then whisk it into the egg and sugar mixture, and cook for a further 5–8 minutes, stirring. Remove from the heat and cool. Cut the passion fruit in half and scoop out the juice and seeds into a bowl. When the custard is cold, stir in the passion fruit juice and seeds and spoon into the pastry case. Chill for 3 hours.

About 30 minutes before you serve, sprinkle 2 tbsp icing sugar over the custard and blowtorch until melted, then repeat with the remaining sugar and blowtorch again until the sugar is browned and bubbling. Chill the tart for 20 minutes until the caramelized topping is crisp.

IF YOU DON'T HAVE A BLOWTORCH, PROTECT THE EDGES OF THE PASTRY WITH SOME FOIL, PREHEAT THE GRILL UNTIL VERY HOT AND BRÛLÉ UNDER THE GRILL. THE BRULÉE TOPPING WILL SOFTEN IF THE TART IS NOT EATEN WITHIN AN HOUR. IT WILL LOSE ITS CRISPNESS BUT IT STILL TASTES DELICIOUS.

TROPICAL FRUIT TART

SERVES 6

Pastry

125 g/4½ oz plain flour

pinch of salt

75 g/2½ oz cold butter, cut into pieces

1 tsp icing sugar

cold water

Filling

2 pieces or 6 g/¼ oz fine leaf gelatine

cold water

210 ml/7 fl oz unsweetened coconut cream

75 g/2½ oz caster sugar

420 ml/15 fl oz double cream

Selection of tropical fruits, such as mango, papaya, passion fruit, Cape gooseberries, pineapple and banana, peeled, prepared and cut into bite-sized pieces.

Lightly butter a 22-cm/9-inch loose-bottomed fluted tart tin. Sift the flour and salt into a food processor, add the butter and process until the mixture resembles fine breadcrumbs. Tip the mixture into a large bowl, stir in the sugar and add a little cold water, just enough to bring the dough together. Turn out on to a floured surface and roll out the pastry 8 cm/3¼ inches larger than the tin. Carefully lift the pastry into the tin and press to fit. Roll the rolling pin over the tin to neaten the edges and trim the excess pastry. Fit a piece of baking paper into the tart case, fill with baking beans and chill in the refrigerator for 30 minutes. Meanwhile, preheat the oven to 190°C/375°F/Gas Mark 5.

Remove the pastry case from the refrigerator and bake the tart case blind for 20 minutes in the preheated oven then remove the beans and paper. Return to the oven for 10 minutes then remove and cool completely.

Soak the gelatine in a little cold water while you heat the coconut cream and caster sugar in a small saucepan. When soft, lift the gelatine out of the water and stir into the hot coconut cream until dissolved. Cool. Whisk the double cream until stiff and fold in the cold coconut mixture, spoon into the tart case and chill for 3 hours. Arrange a colourful pile of the fruit on top of the coconut cream.

Make sure you use plenty of fruit. This is meant to be a decadent dessert and as the coconut cream is quite delicate you need the sweetness of the fruit to complement it. Fresh coconut, pared with a potato peeler, makes a delicious extra topping for this tart.

FIG, RICOTTA & HONEY TART

SERVES 6

Pastry

125 g/4¹/₂ oz plain flour

pinch of salt

75 g/2¹/₂ oz cold butter, cut into pieces

25 g/1 oz ground almonds

cold water

Filling

6 figs

100 g/3¹/₂ oz caster sugar

600 ml/1 pint water

500 g/1 lb 2 oz ricotta cheese

4 egg yolks

¹/₂ tsp vanilla extract

2 tbsp flower honey, plus 1 tsp for drizzling

Lightly butter a 22-cm/9-inch loose-bottomed fluted tart tin. Sift the flour and salt into a food processor, add the butter and process until the mixture resembles fine breadcrumbs. Tip the mixture into a large bowl, stir in the almonds and add a little cold water, just enough to bring the dough together. Turn out on to a floured surface and roll out the pastry 8 cm/3¹/₄ inches larger than the tin. Carefully lift the pastry into the tin and press to fit. Roll the rolling pin over the tin to neaten the edges and trim the excess pastry. Fit a piece of baking paper into the tart case, fill with baking beans and chill for 30 minutes. Meanwhile, preheat the oven to 190°C/375°F/Gas Mark 5.

Remove the pastry case from the refrigerator and bake the tart case blind for 15 minutes in the preheated oven then remove the beans and paper. Return to the oven for 5 minutes.

Put the figs, half the caster sugar and the water in a saucepan and bring to the boil. Poach gently for 10 minutes, drain and cool. Drain any

liquid from the ricotta and stir in the egg yolks and vanilla extract, add the remaining sugar and the honey and mix well. Spoon into the tart case and bake for 30 minutes. Remove from the oven and, when you are ready to serve, cut the figs in half lengthways and arrange on the tart, cut-side up. Drizzle with the extra honey and serve immediately.

IF THE FIGS ARE VERY RIPE YOU COULD SKIP THE POACHING PROCESS: SIMPLY SLICE THE FIGS AND COVER THE SURFACE OF THE TART COMPLETELY, DRIZZLING WITH HONEY.

APPLE GALETTE
WITH CALVADOS CREAM

SERVES 6

Pastry

175 g/6 oz plain flour

pinch of salt

175 g/6 oz cold butter

about 150 ml/5 fl oz chilled water

(or use 250 g/9 oz ready-made puff pastry)

Topping

500 g/1 lb 2 oz Cox's Orange Pippin or other firm, sweet apples

4 tbsp caster sugar

50 g/1¾ oz butter

1 egg, beaten

150 ml/5 fl oz double cream

1 tbsp Calvados

To make the puff pastry sift the flour and salt into a large mixing bowl and rub in 25 g/1 oz butter. Gradually add the water, just enough to bring the pastry together, and knead briefly to form a smooth dough. Wrap the dough in clingfilm and chill for 30 minutes. Keep the remaining butter out of the refrigerator, wrap in a piece of clingfilm and shape it into a 3-cm/1¼-inch thick rectangle. Roll out the dough to a rectangle 3 times longer and 3 cm/1¼ inches wider than the butter and place the butter in the centre, long-side towards you. Fold over the 2 'wings' of pastry to enclose the butter – press down the edges to seal and then turn the pastry so the short side faces you. Roll the pastry to its original length, fold into 3, turn and roll again to its original length. Repeat this once more then rewrap the pastry and chill again for 30 minutes. Remove from the refrigerator and repeat the rolling and turning twice more. Chill again for 30 minutes. At this point you can freeze the pastry until you need it.

ALMONDS WORK VERY WELL WITH APPLES SO AN ALTERNATIVE WOULD BE TO SCATTER THE COOKED TART WITH TOASTED, FLAKED ALMONDS AND USE AN ALMOND LIQUEUR INSTEAD OF THE CALVADOS IN THE CREAM.

Peel, core and thinly slice the apples. Heat the sugar and butter in a frying pan, add the apples and cook gently for 10–15 minutes. Cool. Preheat the oven to 200°C/400°F/Gas Mark 6. Roll out the pastry to a large rectangle and place on a baking tray. Lift the apples from the pan with a slotted spoon and arrange in neat rows on the pastry, leaving a 3-cm/1¼-inch margin around the edge of the pastry. Brush the pastry with the egg and bake for 30–35 minutes. Reheat the apple butter syrup and reduce until it is thick then use it to brush over the apples. Whip the cream, stir in the Calvados and chill. Serve the hot tart with the cold Calvados cream.

POACHED PEAR TART
WITH MARSALA SYLLABUB

SERVES 6

Pastry

125 g/4¹/₂ oz plain flour

pinch of salt

75 g/2¹/₂ oz cold butter, cut into pieces

1 tsp icing sugar

cold water

Filling

2 firm pears, peeled, cored and halved

1 large strip lemon rind

200 ml/7 fl oz Marsala or Madeira

175 g/6 oz caster sugar

100 ml/3¹/₂ fl oz water

175 g/6 oz butter

3 eggs

200 g/7 oz ground almonds

50 g/1³/₄ oz plain flour

Marsala Syllabub

120 ml/4 fl oz Marsala

125 g/4¹/₂ oz caster sugar

1 cinnamon stick

240 ml/8 fl oz double cream

Lightly butter a 22-cm/9-inch loose-bottomed fluted tart tin. Sift the flour and salt into a food processor, add the butter and process until the mixture resembles fine breadcrumbs. Tip the mixture into a large bowl, stir in the sugar and add a little cold water, just enough to bring the dough together. Turn out on to a floured surface and roll out the pastry 8 cm/3¹/₄ inches larger than the tin. Carefully lift the pastry into the tin and press to fit. Roll the rolling pin over the tin

THE SYLLABUB COULD BE FLAVOURED WITH CALVADOS OR POIRE WILLIAM. IT ALSO WORKS WELL SPOONED OVER POACHED FRUITS AND SERVED WITH LITTLE SWEET BISCUITS.

to neaten the edges and trim the excess pastry. Fit a piece of baking paper into the tart case, fill with baking beans and chill in the refrigerator for 30 minutes. Meanwhile, preheat the oven to 190°C/375°F/Gas Mark 5.

Remove the pastry case from the refrigerator and bake blind for 10 minutes in the preheated oven then remove the beans and paper. Return to the oven for 5 minutes.

Put the pears, lemon rind, Marsala, 2 tbsp of the sugar and the water in a saucepan and bring up to the boil. Simmer for 30 minutes, or until the pears are tender. Leave in the liquid to cool. Slice the pears lengthways.

Melt 150 g/5¹/₂ oz of the butter. Beat the remaining sugar with the eggs and stir in the melted butter and then the almonds and flour. Pour the almond mixture into the pastry case and arrange the pear slices in a cartwheel pattern on top. Melt the remaining butter and brush it over the pears. Bake for 25–30 minutes. Meanwhile, put the Marsala, sugar and cinnamon stick for the syllabub in a saucepan and simmer for 5 minutes. Strain and cool.

When you are ready to serve, make the syllabub. Put the cooled Marsala in a bowl and gradually whip in the cream with an electric whisk until soft peaks form. Slice the tart and spoon a good dollop of syllabub on each slice.

The tarts in this chapter come into the category of indulgence because of their rich and luxurious fillings and glamorous appearance. An elegant tart is always an impressive end to a special dinner. The pastry for these tarts tends to be fairly plain as it is the fillings that are making the statement, but adding an egg yolk to the pastry will make it richer, while adding 15 g/½ oz of very finely ground amaretti biscuits will add an almond crunch to the pastry. One large tart looks impressive in terms of presentation but all the tarts in this chapter can be made as individual tarts – people often prefer their own tartlet because they don't have to restrict themselves to one small, self-restrained slice.

Sweet tarts are the perfect excuse for decadent fillings and if you are going to town with a rich filling it really is essential to use the best ingredients you can find: dark chocolate

PART FOUR
SWEET INDULGENCE

LUXURIOUS, RICH
DESSERT TARTS

with the highest cocoa solids content – at least 70% is a must for the Fine Chocolate Tart – and undyed, natural glacé cherries for the Florentine Tarts.

These very rich sweet tarts are usually enough served on their own but if you need a little something extra offer chilled double cream for pouring.

For a party make both the dark chocolate and the white chocolate tarts and serve with a bowl of loganberries or raspberries – a combination that looks very elegant and enticing. For a smart dinner make these as individual small tartlets and give each guest one white and one dark chocolate tartlet and a few berries.

FINE CHOCOLATE TART

SERVES 6

Pastry

125 g/4¹/₂ oz plain flour

2 tsp cocoa powder

2 tsp icing sugar

pinch of salt

50 g/1³/₄ oz cold butter, cut into pieces

1 egg yolk

ice-cold water

Ganache Filling

200 g/7 oz plain chocolate with 70% cocoa solids

25 g/1 oz unsalted butter, softened

240 ml/8 fl oz double cream

1 tsp dark rum (optional)

Lightly butter a 22-cm/9-inch loose-bottomed fluted tart tin. Sift the flour, cocoa powder, icing sugar and salt into a food processor, add the butter and process until the mixture resembles fine breadcrumbs. Tip the mixture into a large bowl, add the egg yolk and add a little ice-cold water, just enough to bring the dough together. Turn out on to a surface dusted with more flour and cocoa powder and roll out the pastry 8 cm/ 3¹/₄ inches larger than the tin. Carefully lift the pastry into the tin and press to fit. Roll the rolling pin over the tin to neaten the edges and trim the excess pastry. Fit a piece of baking paper into the tart case, fill with baking beans and chill in the refrigerator for 30 minutes. Meanwhile, preheat the oven to 190°C/375°F/Gas Mark 5.

Remove the pastry case from the refrigerator and bake the pastry for 15 minutes in the preheated oven then remove the beans and paper and bake for a further 5 minutes.

To make the ganache filling, chop the chocolate and put in a bowl with the softened butter. Bring the cream to the boil then pour on to the chocolate, stirring well, add the rum (if using) and continue stirring to make sure the chocolate is melted completely. Pour into the pastry case and chill for 3 hours.

IF LIKED, SIFT MORE COCOA POWDER OVER THE SURFACE OF THE TART OR, FOR SERIOUS CHOCOHOLICS, CRUSH A HANDFUL OF CHOCOLATE-COATED COFFEE BEANS AND SPRINKLE OVER THE SURFACE. A BOWL OF CRÈME FRAÎCHE IS A LOVELY ACCOMPANIMENT FOR THIS TART.

TRUFFLED HONEY TART

SERVES 6

Pastry

125 g/4¹/₂ oz plain flour

pinch of salt

75 g/2¹/₂ oz cold butter, cut into pieces

1 tsp icing sugar

cold water

Filling

250 g/9 oz curd cheese

100 g/3¹/₂ oz cream cheese

120 ml/4 fl oz double cream

2 egg yolks, plus 1 whole egg

25 g/1 oz caster sugar

4 tbsp flower honey, plus extra for drizzling

crystallized violets or sugared rose petals, to decorate

Lightly butter a 22-cm/9-inch loose-bottomed fluted tart tin. Sift the flour and salt into a food processor, add the butter and process until the mixture resembles fine breadcrumbs. Tip the mixture into a large bowl, add the sugar and a little cold water, just enough to bring the dough together. Turn out on to a surface dusted with more flour and roll out the pastry 8 cm/ 3¹/₄ inches larger than the tin. Carefully lift the pastry into the tin and press to fit. Roll the rolling pin over the tin to neaten the edges and trim the excess pastry. Fit a piece of baking paper into the tart case, fill with baking beans and chill in the refrigerator for 30 minutes. Meanwhile, preheat the oven to 190°C/375°F/Gas Mark 5.

Remove the pastry case from the refrigerator and bake blind for 10 minutes in the preheated oven then remove the beans and paper and bake for a further 5 minutes.

USE YOUR FAVOURITE HONEY – FLOWER HONEY, SUCH AS LAVENDER, WORKS WELL, AS DOES CHESTNUT HONEY. ALTERNATIVE TOPPINGS TO SCATTER OVER INCLUDE PISTACHIO NUTS ROLLED IN HONEY OR ROUGHLY CRUSHED HONEYCOMB.

Mix the curd cheese, cream cheese and cream together until smooth then stir in the egg yolks and whole egg plus the sugar and honey until completely smooth. Pour into the pastry case and bake for 30 minutes. Remove from the oven and cool in the tin for 10 minutes. Drizzle with more honey and decorate with violets or petals.

WHITE CHOCOLATE & CARDAMOM TART

SERVES 6

Pastry

125 g/4¹/₂ oz plain flour

pinch of salt

75 g/2¹/₂ oz cold butter, cut into pieces

cold water

Filling

2 pieces or 6 g/¹/₄ oz fine leaf gelatine

cold water

seeds of 8 cardamom pods

350 g/12 oz white chocolate, chopped into small pieces

390 ml/13 fl oz whipping cream

Lightly butter a 22-cm/9-inch loose-bottomed fluted tart tin. Sift the flour and salt into a food processor, add the butter and process until the mixture resembles fine breadcrumbs. Tip the mixture into a large bowl and add a little cold water, just enough to bring the dough together. Turn out on to a surface dusted with more flour and roll out the pastry 8 cm/3¹/₄ inches larger than the tin. Carefully lift the pastry into the tin and press to fit. Roll the rolling pin over the tin to neaten the edges and trim the excess pastry. Fit a piece of baking paper into the tart case, fill with baking beans and chill for 30 minutes. Meanwhile, preheat the oven to 190°C/375°F/Gas Mark 5.

Remove the pastry case from the refrigerator and bake blind for 15 minutes in the preheated oven then remove the beans and paper and bake for a further 10 minutes. Cool completely.

Soak the gelatine in a little cold water in a small heatproof bowl for 5 minutes. Heat a saucepan of water to simmering point. Crush the cardamom seeds until powdery and put in a large bowl with the chocolate. Place the bowl of gelatine over the saucepan of simmering water and stir until dissolved. At the same time, in a separate saucepan, heat the cream until just boiling then pour over the chocolate, using a whisk to stir the chocolate until it has melted. Add the gelatine and stir until the mixture is smooth. Cool and pour into the tart case then chill for at least 3 hours.

YOU COULD SERVE THIS TART DECORATED WITH WHITE CHOCOLATE CURLS OR SIMPLY SIFT A LITTLE COCOA POWDER OVER THE WHITE CHOCOLATE BEFORE SERVING. EDIBLE FLOWER PETALS SCATTERED OVER THE SURFACE MAKE A PRETTY DECORATION, TOO.

SICILIAN MARZIPAN
TART WITH CANDIED FRUIT

SERVES 6

Pastry

125 g/4¹/2 oz plain flour

pinch of salt

75 g/2¹/2 oz cold butter, cut into pieces

cold water

Filling

300 g/10¹/2 oz marzipan

175 g/6 oz ground almonds

150 g/5¹/2 oz unsalted butter

100 g/3¹/2 oz caster sugar

75 g/2¹/2 oz plain flour

2 eggs

75 g/3 oz sultanas

50 g/1³/4 oz mixed candied peel, chopped

75 g/2¹/2 oz natural glacé cherries, halved

50 g/1³/4 oz flaked almonds

Lightly butter a 22-cm/9-inch loose-bottomed fluted tart tin. Sift the flour and salt into a food processor, add the butter and process until the mixture resembles fine breadcrumbs. Tip the mixture into a large bowl and add a little cold water, just enough to bring the dough together. Turn out on to a surface dusted with more flour and roll out the pastry 8 cm/3¹/4 inches larger than the tin. Carefully lift the pastry into the tin and press to fit. Roll the rolling pin over the tin to neaten the edges and trim the excess pastry. Fit a piece of baking paper into the tart case, fill with baking beans and chill for 30 minutes.

Meanwhile, preheat the oven to 190°C/375°F/ Gas Mark 5.

Remove the pastry case from the refrigerator and bake blind for 10 minutes in the preheated oven then remove the beans and paper and bake for a further 5 minutes.

Reduce the oven temperature to 180°C/350°F/Gas Mark 4. Grate the marzipan straight on to the base of the warm pastry, distributing evenly. Put the ground almonds, butter and sugar in a food processor and pulse until smooth. Add 1 tbsp flour and 1 of the eggs and blend then add another 1 tbsp flour and the other egg and blend. Finally add the remaining flour. Scoop the mixture into a bowl and stir in the sultanas, peel and cherries. Spoon the mixture over the marzipan, scatter with the flaked almonds and bake for 40 minutes.

SERVE WARM WITH SINGLE CREAM OR WHISK A LITTLE ALMOND LIQUEUR AND ICING SUGAR INTO MASCARPONE CHEESE. A GLASS OF SICILIAN DESSERT WINE IS DELICIOUS WITH THIS TART.

BRANDIED PLUM TART

Serves 6

Pastry

125g/4¹/2 oz plain flour

pinch of salt

75 g/2¹/2 oz cold butter, cut into pieces

cold water

Filling

150 ml/5 fl oz brandy or Armagnac

100 g/3¹/2 oz golden caster sugar

4–5 ripe but not soft plums, halved

1 whole egg, plus 2 egg yolks

300 ml/10 fl oz double cream

Lightly butter a 22-cm/9-inch loose-bottomed fluted tart tin. Sift the flour and salt into a food processor, add the butter and process until the mixture resembles fine breadcrumbs. Tip the mixture into a large bowl and add a little cold water, just enough to bring the dough together. Turn out on to a surface dusted with more flour and roll out the pastry 8 cm/3¹/4 inches larger than the tin. Carefully lift the pastry into the tin and press to fit. Roll the rolling pin over the tin to neaten the edges and trim the excess pastry. Fit a piece of baking paper into the tart case, fill with baking beans and chill for 30 minutes. Meanwhile, preheat the oven to 190°C/375°F/Gas Mark 5.

Remove the pastry case from the refrigerator and bake blind for 10 minutes in the preheated oven then remove the beans and paper and bake for a further 5 minutes.

Put the brandy and 2 tbsp of the sugar in a saucepan and bring to a simmer, making sure the sugar has dissolved. Add the plum halves and simmer for 5 minutes then set aside to cool. Reduce the oven temperature to 160°C/325°F/Gas Mark 3.

Lift the plums out of the syrup with a slotted spoon, reserving the syrup. Slip the skins off the plums and slice each half plum into 3–4 slices, arranging the slices in the bottom of the pastry case. Beat the egg and the egg yolks with the remaining sugar and heat the cream until just boiling. Whisk the hot cream into the eggs, stirring constantly. Spoon the custard over the plums, return the tart to the oven and cook for 30–40 minutes, until the custard is set. Leave in the tin until completely cold then carefully lift on to a serving plate. Serve with the reserved syrup in a small jug to drizzle over.

THIS TART IS EASILY ADAPTED. USE CHERRIES, APRICOTS OR STEWED RHUBARB IF YOU DON'T WANT TO USE PLUMS. YOU COULD ALSO USE A FRUIT COMPOTE OR HOME-MADE JAM.

FLORENTINE PRALINE TARTLETS

MAKES 6 TARTLETS

Praline

100 g/3¹/₂ oz sugar

3 tbsp water

50 g/1³/₄ oz flaked almonds

butter

Pastry

125 g/4¹/₂ oz plain flour

pinch of salt

75 g/2¹/₂ oz cold butter, cut into pieces

1 tsp icing sugar

cold water

Frangipane

75 g/2¹/₂ oz butter

2 eggs

75 g/2¹/₂ oz caster sugar

25 g/1 oz plain flour

100 g/3¹/₂ oz ground almonds

Topping

8 natural glacé cherries, chopped

25 g/1 oz mixed candied peel, chopped

100 g/3¹/₂ oz plain chocolate, chopped

First make the praline. Put the sugar and the water in a saucepan and dissolve the sugar over a low heat. Do not stir the sugar, just let it boil for 10 minutes, until it turns to caramel, then stir in the nuts and turn out on to buttered foil. Allow to cool and harden. When cold break up the praline and chop into smallish pieces.

Butter 6 x 9-cm/3¹/₂-inch loose-bottomed fluted tart tins. Sift the flour and salt into a food processor, add the butter and process until the mixture resembles fine breadcrumbs. Tip the mixture into a large bowl, add the sugar and a little cold water, just enough to bring the dough together. Turn out on to a floured surface and divide into 6 equal-sized pieces. Roll each piece to fit the tart tins. Carefully fit each piece of pastry in its case and press well to fit the tin. Roll the rolling pin over the tin to neaten the edges and trim the excess pastry. Put in the freezer for 30 minutes. Meanwhile, preheat the oven to 200°C/400°F/Gas Mark 6.

YOU CAN SUBSTITUTE WHITE OR MILK CHOCOLATE FOR THE PLAIN CHOCOLATE OR USE DRIED FIGS OR APRICOTS INSTEAD OF THE CANDIED PEEL. A LITTLE CHOPPED STEM GINGER IS ALSO VERY GOOD ADDED TO THE TOPPING.

While the tarts are in the freezer, make the frangipane. Melt the butter and beat the eggs and sugar together. Stir the melted butter into the egg and sugar mixture, then add the flour and almonds. Bake the tart cases blind, straight from the freezer, for 10 minutes in the preheated oven. Divide the frangipane among the tart shells and return to the oven for 8–10 minutes. Cool completely.

While the tarts are baking, mix the cherries, peel, chocolate and praline together. Divide among the tarts while they are still hot so that some of the chocolate melts. Serve cold.

PANNA COTTA TARTLETS WITH STRAWBERRY COMPOTE

MAKES 6 TARTLETS

Pastry

125 g/4¹/₂ oz plain flour

pinch of salt

75 g/2¹/₂ oz cold butter, cut into pieces

1 tsp icing sugar

cold water

Compote

500 g/1 lb 2 oz fresh strawberries, hulled and quartered

1 tsp caster sugar or 1 tsp flower honey

1 tsp orange flower water (optional)

Filling

1 vanilla pod

50 g/1³/₄ oz caster sugar

270 ml/9 fl oz double cream

1¹/₂ pieces or 4 g/¹/₃ oz leaf gelatine

cold water

icing sugar, to serve

Butter 6 x 9-cm/3¹/₂-inch loose-bottomed fluted tart tins. Sift the flour and salt into a food processor, add the butter and process until the mixture resembles fine breadcrumbs. Tip the mixture into a large bowl, add the sugar and a little cold water, just enough to bring the dough together. Turn out on to a floured surface and divide into 6 equal-sized pieces. Roll each piece to fit the tartlet tins. Carefully fit each piece of pastry in its case and press well to fit the tin. Roll the rolling pin over the tin to neaten the edges and trim the excess pastry. Put in the freezer for 30 minutes. Meanwhile, preheat the oven to 200°C/400°F/Gas Mark 6. Bake the tart cases blind, straight from the freezer, for 15 minutes in the preheated oven. Cool the tart cases completely, carefully remove from the tins and transfer to a serving plate.

To make the compote, heat the strawberries in a saucepan with the sugar or honey and flower water, if using. When the fruits start to break down, reduce the heat and simmer for 2–3 minutes. Cool completely.

To make the filling, split the vanilla pod lengthways and put into a saucepan with the sugar and half the cream. Bring gently to a simmer. Meanwhile, soak the gelatine in a little cold water. When the cream is very hot remove the vanilla pod, lift the gelatine from the water and stir into the cream until completely dissolved. Scrape the vanilla seeds into the warm cream and stir again. Leave to cool. (Wipe the vanilla pod dry and use in another recipe).

Whisk the remaining cream until it begins to thicken then fold the creams together. Chill until cold, spoon into the pastry cases and chill for 2 hours. When ready to serve, spoon the strawberry compote on to the tarts and sift a little icing sugar on top.

FRESH FRUIT COMPOTE CAN BE MADE BY ADDING A LITTLE HONEY OR SUGAR TO BERRIES OR SLICED STONED FRUITS SUCH AS PEACHES, APRICOTS OR PLUMS, ADDING A LITTLE COMPLEMENTARY LIQUOR, AND SIMMERING UNTIL SOFT. CHILL UNTIL NEEDED.

CARAMELIZED LEMON TART

SERVES 6

Pastry

175 g/6 oz plain flour

pinch of salt

100 g/3½ oz cold butter, cut into pieces

25 g/1 oz caster sugar

1 egg yolk

cold water

Filling

5 lemons

2 eggs

300 g/10½ oz caster sugar

150 g/5½ oz ground almonds

100 ml/3½ fl oz whipping cream

100 ml/3½ fl oz water

Lightly butter a 22-cm/9-inch loose-bottomed fluted tart tin. Sift the flour and salt into a food processor, add the butter and process until the mixture resembles fine breadcrumbs. Tip the mixture into a large bowl, add the sugar and egg yolk and a little cold water, just enough to bring the dough together. Turn out on to a surface dusted with more flour and roll out the pastry 8 cm/3¼ inches larger than the tin. Carefully lift the pastry into the tin and press to fit. Roll the rolling pin over the tin to neaten the edges and trim the excess pastry. Fit a piece of baking paper into the tart case, fill with baking beans and chill in the refrigerator for 30 minutes. Meanwhile, preheat the oven to 190°C/375°F/Gas Mark 5.

Remove the pastry case from the refrigerator and bake blind for 10 minutes in the preheated oven then remove the beans and paper and bake for a further 5 minutes.

THE GROUND ALMONDS IN THE FILLING MAKE THIS A RATHER SUBSTANTIAL TART, QUITE DIFFERENT FROM THE SMOOTH-TEXTURED CLASSIC FRENCH TARTE AU CITRON. THE STICKY LEMON SLICES ON THE TOP MEAN THIS TART WILL NOT SLICE NEATLY – BUT IT IS SO DELICIOUS THAT NO ONE WILL MIND.

Put the juice and finely grated rind of 3 of the lemons in a large bowl and add the eggs, 100 g/3½ oz of the sugar, the ground almonds and the cream, whisking to combine. Pour into the pastry case and bake for 25 minutes. Meanwhile, thinly slice the remaining 2 lemons, discarding the pips and ends. Put the remaining sugar and water in a saucepan and heat until the sugar is melted. Simmer for 5 minutes then add the lemon slices and boil for 10 minutes.

Remove the tart from the oven and arrange the lemon slices over the surface in a spiral pattern. Drizzle the remaining lemon syrup over the slices. Serve warm or cold, with whipped cream.

CHESTNUT, MAPLE SYRUP & PECAN TART

SERVES 6

Pastry

125 g/4¹/₂ oz plain flour

pinch of salt

75 g/2¹/₂ oz cold butter, cut into pieces

cold water

Filling

1 kg/2 lb 4 oz canned sweetened chestnut purée

300 ml/10 fl oz double cream

25 g/1 oz butter

2 tbsp maple syrup

150 g/5¹/₂ oz pecan nuts

Lightly butter a 22-cm/9-inch loose-bottomed fluted tart tin. Sift the flour and salt into a food processor, add the butter and process until the mixture resembles fine breadcrumbs. Tip the mixture into a large bowl and add a little cold water, just enough to bring the dough together. Turn out on to a surface dusted with more flour and roll out the pastry 8 cm/3¹/₄ inches larger than the tin. Carefully lift the pastry into the tin and press to fit. Roll the rolling pin over the tin to neaten the edges and trim the excess pastry. Fit a piece of baking paper into the tart case, fill with baking beans and chill in the refrigerator for 30 minutes. Meanwhile, preheat the oven to 190°C/ 375°F/Gas Mark 5.

Remove the pastry case from the refrigerator and bake for 15 minutes then remove the beans and paper and bake for a further 10 minutes.

Empty the chestnut purée into a large bowl. Whip the cream until stiff and fold into the chestnut purée. Spoon into the cold pastry case and chill for 2 hours. Melt the butter with the maple syrup and when bubbling add the pecans and stir for 1–2 minutes. Spoon on to baking paper and cool. When ready to serve, arrange the pecans on the chestnut cream.

THIS TART IS VERY RICH AND SWEET. IF YOU WOULD PREFER IT LESS SWEET, REPLACE HALF OF THE SWEETENED CHESTNUT PURÉE WITH UNSWEETENED, AND ADD MAPLE SYRUP TO TASTE UNTIL THE MIXTURE IS THE SWEETNESS YOU LIKE.

ORANGE MARMALADE
CUSTARD TART

SERVES 6

Pastry

125 g/4¹/2 oz plain flour

pinch of salt

75 g/2¹/2 oz cold butter,
cut into pieces

1 egg yolk

finely grated rind of
¹/2 orange

cold water

Filling

3 tbsp orange marmalade

1 egg, plus 3 egg yolks

100 g/3¹/2 oz caster sugar

390 ml/13 fl oz double
cream

finely grated rind of
1 orange and the juice
of ¹/2 orange

¹/2 tsp orange flower
water (optional)

To decorate

finely grated orange rind

icing sugar

Lightly butter a 22-cm/9-inch loose-bottomed fluted tart tin. Sift the flour and salt into a food processor, add the butter and process until the mixture resembles fine breadcrumbs. Tip the mixture into a large bowl, add the egg yolk and orange rind and a little cold water, just enough to bring the dough together. Turn out on to a surface dusted with more flour and roll out the pastry 8 cm/3¹/4 inches larger than the tin. Carefully lift the pastry into the tin and press to fit. Roll the rolling pin over the tin to neaten the edges and trim the excess pastry. Fit a piece of baking paper into the tart case, fill with baking beans and chill in the refrigerator for 30 minutes. Preheat the oven to 190°C/375°F/Gas Mark 5.

Remove the pastry case from the refrigerator and bake blind for 10 minutes in the preheated oven then remove the beans and paper and bake for a further 5 minutes.

Reduce the oven to 160°C/325°F/Gas Mark 3. Spread the marmalade over the bottom of the pastry case. Beat the egg, egg yolks and sugar together and heat the cream until simmering. Pour the hot cream over the egg mixture, whisking to combine, then add the orange rind, orange juice and orange flower water (if using) and stir well. Pour on top of the marmalade and bake for 40–45 minutes. Serve cold.

INSTEAD OF THE ORANGE FLOWER WATER YOU CAN USE COINTREAU OR ANOTHER ORANGE-FLAVOURED LIQUEUR AND SERVE A GLASS OF IT WITH THE TART ALONG WITH SOME CHILLED POURING CREAM.

INDEX